Gillen.

This booklet was written by the research team at GillenMarkets. It is also available in eBook format (PDF, ePub or Kindle).

About Gillen

Gillen is a boutique investment advisor offering expert advice on the management of personal, pension and corporate monies. We place a strong emphasis on fully understanding our clients' needs, so that we can make informed decisions and plans, together.

We are investment advisors, not product sellers. Our investment solutions are structured to meet the specific needs of each individual client with minimum assets of €500k.

Our investment advisory fee structure aligns our interests with yours, ensuring that we sit on the same side of the table as our clients.

With our fee structure, there are:

- No upfront commissions or fees payable by clients.
- No dealing costs.
- No early redemption penalties.
- No VAT.

Just a transparent 1.0% annual advisory fee on the assets under advice.

We also offer a subscription-based investment newsletter for do-it-yourself investors and training courses both in-person and online for those wishing to learn more about the principles of sound investing.

We believe trust is earned. Our belief is that we work for clients, looking at each individual's needs and taking a common-sense, long-term approach.

We have built an outstanding team with the depth of knowledge and experience to meet all our clients' investment needs. We have an appetite for learning and sharing and we always partner with our clients as equals.

We'd like to hear from you!

Contact details

T: + 353 (0)1 287 1400
E: info@gillenmarkets.com
W: www.gillenmarkets.com

Follow us on Facebook, LinkedIn, Twitter and Gillenmarkets.com.

ILTB Ltd (trading as Gillen/GillenMarkets) is regulated by the Central Bank of Ireland.

Iconic Consumer Brands for More Defensive, Lower-risk Investing

Annual Review 2023

Darren Gillen & Jonathan Yates

OAK·TREE·PRESS

Published by OAK TREE PRESS, Cork T12 XY2N
www.oaktreepress.com / www.SuccessStore.com

© 2023 ILTB Ltd t/a GillenMarkets

A catalogue record of this book is available from the British Library.

ISBN 978 1 78119 618 2 (Paperback)
ISBN 978 1 78119 619 9 (PDF)
ISBN 978 1 78119 620 5 (ePub)
ISBN 978 1 78119 621 2 (Kindle)

Disclaimer

Investing carries risk and none of the stocks or funds highlighted in this booklet constitute a recommendation by the author, GillenMarkets or the publisher and none of these parties can assume liability for any losses that may be sustained should a reader subsequently invest in them, and any such liability is hereby disclaimed. Readers should take professional advice before making any investment. None of the material in this publication constitutes investment advice or an offer to invest in any of the funds referred to. No one receiving this publication should treat it as a personal recommendation as it does not take into account the needs and objectives, personal circumstances, including investment experience, financial position, or attitude to risk of recipients.

Warning

Past performance is not a reliable guide to future performance.

CONTENTS

Gillen.

INTRODUCTION

Here is a test: below is a list of famous consumer brands. Can you tell what they have in common?

Jack Daniel's - Coca-Cola - Colgate - Corona - Listerine - McDonald's - Cadbury - Gillette - Head & Shoulders - Guinness - Sensodyne - Heineken - Nescafé - Dove - Vaseline - Ben & Jerry's.

The answer is: they are all owned by one of the eight US and six European companies that make up GillenMarkets' Defensive Global Consumer Franchise Stocks Theme. An extensive list, to be sure – and yet, it barely scratches the surface of these companies' extensive brand portfolios.

Through a focus on high-quality manufacturing and decades (if not centuries) of savvy marketing, these brands occupy a highly esteemed and trusted place in a consumer's mind. Their status as low-ticket, everyday essentials or small luxuries means that consumers are often loathe to give them up, or substitute them with an alternative brand or generic product.

Ownership of these irreplaceable brands confers several advantages potent enough to make any competitor jealous. These companies' sales and profits tend to be defensive during recessions, because they are essential items, or affordable luxuries. Because they are low-ticket, everyday, repeat purchases, their sales and profits tend to be predictable. And, finally, because they are irreplaceable in consumers' minds, they can often raise prices without losing customers.

Defensive. Predictable. Inflation-resistant. An utterly enviable set of attributes!

We cover the theme because it offers, we believe, a balanced alternative between the higher risks associated with general equity investing and the safety of risk-free government bonds.

Defensive, predictable, and inflation-resistant sales and profits mean that these companies' earnings are less volatile than general industry (and thus less risky). That is why we compare them to the regular, risk-free income and return of principal available from government bonds. However, unlike government bonds, these companies can grow their earnings and dividends over time.

We have covered the theme for 13 years now, and the companies themselves have been around a lot longer than that. They have survived wars and plagues – and not just survived, but prospered.

What better way for the risk-averse investor, who nonetheless wants a reasonable return on their capital, to invest?

SUMMARY

Our US & European Defensive Global Consumer Franchise Stocks (DGCFS) Theme has been running since late-May 2010 and offers investors a middle ground between the higher risks of general equity investing and risk-free government bonds.

The stocks in the theme are shown in *Table 1* and include eight US and six European companies.

Table 1: Stocks in the US & European Defensive Global Consumer Franchise Stocks Theme

US	European
Brown Forman	Diageo
Coca-Cola	Haleon
Colgate-Palmolive	Heineken
Constellation Brands	Nestlé
Kenvue	Reckitt
McDonald's	Unilever
Mondelēz International	
Procter & Gamble	

The theme involves investing in companies that have strong consumer brands, global reach and are selling products that are purchased regularly either because they are low-priced everyday essentials or affordable luxuries. These characteristics have in the past led to demand resilience for such companies, providing them with defensive earnings even in recessions. Furthermore, the strength of the brands means that the companies can often pass on the costs of inflation to consumers – a characteristic which has been particularly important over the past 18 months.

As we outline in more detail in **Chapter 1: The Returns Record**, the DGCFS have demonstrable track records of stable, defensive earnings.

Over the 13-year period that the theme has been running, choosing an investment in this basket of stocks over long-dated (risk-free) government bonds has had many advantages. Until recently, US and European long-dated government bonds offered low yields with no possibility of growth in that yield. However, with the advent of rising bond yields (i.e., rising interest rates) in response to higher inflation, government bonds are now a more credible investment proposition.

Nonetheless, we maintain our view that the DGCFS remain an attractive investment opportunity. Offering an initial dividend yield of 2.4%, along with the likelihood of 3% to 5% *per annum* growth in that yield, means that these stocks hold out the prospect of annualised total returns of 5.5% to 7.5% *per annum* over the medium-term from here. This is still a decent risk premium over 10-year government bonds yielding 2.6% (Germany) to 4.2% (US).

Moreover, these stocks have pushed through price increases to offset rising input costs and have achieved this without overly impacting volumes. In other words, revenue and earnings growth come with an element of much-needed inflation protection!

This annual update on the theme is aimed at:

- Providing an understanding of the theme;
- Examining whether the theme still offers sufficient value to underpin reasonable returns from here;
- Recent developments, including how the companies have responded to higher inflation; and
- The changing shape of balance sheets, with long-term debt being locked in at low rates to fund, in part, share buybacks.

We also highlight some fund structures that allow investors to indirectly invest in the theme.

(**Note:** All data is as of 1st September 2023, unless otherwise noted.)

1: THE RETURNS RECORD

The US Theme

The US theme was started in May 2010 and the eight stocks currently included in it are Brown Forman, Coca-Cola, Colgate, Constellation Brands, Kenvue, McDonald's, Mondelēz International, and Procter & Gamble.

The stocks composing the US basket have changed over time. In May 2020, Brown Forman, Clorox, and Constellation Brands were added in order to increase the number of sectors covered. Kenvue was added in August 2023 following its split-off from Johnson & Johnson (which was removed at the same time). Walmart was removed in May 2016 (US-focused), Kellogg in October 2020 (declining core business), Johnson & Johnson (previously mentioned), and Clorox in September 2023 (US-focused business, and doubts about value of core Health & Wellness franchise).

Chart 1: US Theme: Total Returns Comparison (May 2010 – September 2023)

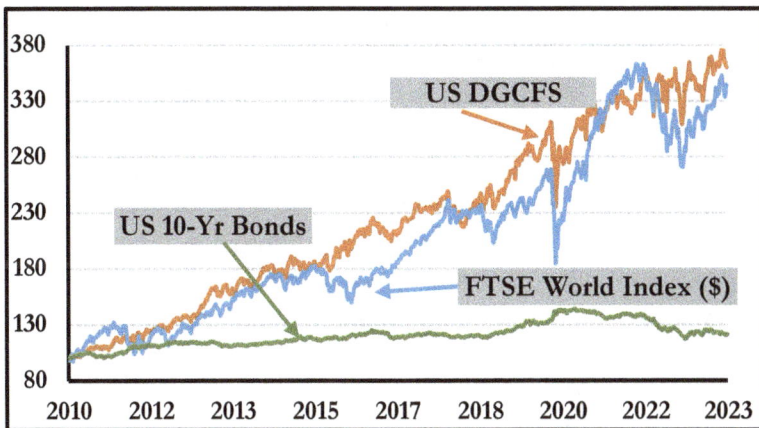

Source: Bloomberg, GillenMarkets.

Chart 1 highlights the returns from the theme from 28th May 2010 to 1st September 2023. The periodic returns are outlined in *Table 2.* The returns assume that an investor in the theme re-balances their portfolio annually to avoid the returns of outsized under- or outperformers skewing the results. Stocks exiting and entering the theme are accounted for from/until the relevant date.

Table 2: US Theme: Total Returns (Income Reinvested)*

Time period	US 10-Yr Bonds	FTSE All-World ($)	US DGCFS
1 Year	-3.1%	12.1%	3.4%
3 Years	-14.6%	24.9%	15.1%
5 Years	0.5%	46.9%	50.8%
10 Years	9.2%	139.6%	128.9%
Since May 2010	21.3%	243.7%	259.4%
Since May 2010 c.p.a.	1.5%	9.8%	10.1%

* Returns in US dollars.   Source: Bloomberg, GillenMarkets.

Income and capital growth from US 10-year government bonds over the May 2010 to September 2023 period delivered an investor a total return of 21.3%, or 1.5% compound *per annum*. These returns were impacted negatively by rising bond yields in 2022, which reduced the capital value of bonds. As we can see from *Table 2*, US 10-year government bond returns were -14.6% over the past 3 years – wiping out a significant portion of the past decade's gains.

In comparison, an investment in the US DGCFS provided a total return of 259.4% (with dividends reinvested), or 10.1% compound *per annum*. These returns exceed those of the FTSE All-World Total Return Index, which delivered 243.7%, or 9.8% compound *per annum*.

It is worth noting that outperformance was strong over the past two years, when the stocks in the theme held up well during a period of declining equity markets. Since global equity markets peaked in November 2021, the US stocks in the theme have returned 7.7%, compared to a return of -5.2% for the FTSE All-World Total Return Index. This reflects, in our view, investors' need for stable, inflation-protected businesses during a period of volatility and high inflation.

The European Theme

The European theme was started later but, for consistency, we also present the returns and earnings data from May 2010 to September 2023.

European stocks in the theme include Diageo, Haleon, Heineken, Nestlé, Reckitt and Unilever. Kerry Group and Henkel were removed from the theme in January 2023 as we thought they were no longer a good fit. Haleon was introduced in January 2023 following its spin-off from GSK.

Chart 2: European Theme: Total Returns Comparison (May 2010 – September 2023)

Source: Bloomberg, GillenMarkets

Chart 2 highlights the returns from these stocks from 28th May 2010 to 1st September 2023 and the periodic returns are outlined in **Table 3**. The returns are calculated in the same way as for the US basket.

Income and capital growth from German 10-year government bonds over the May 2010 to September 2023 period delivered an investor a total return of 22.3%, or 1.5% compound *per annum*. Similar to US government bonds, these returns were impacted negatively by rising bond yields in 2022, which reduced the capital value of bonds. As we can see from the table, German 10-year government bond returns were -19.1% over the past 3 years and -13.9% over the past 5 years – wiping out a significant portion of the past decade's gains.

Table 3: European Theme: Total Returns (Income Reinvested)*

Time Period	German 10-Yr Bonds	FTSE All-World (€)	European DGCFS
1 Year	-5.8%	7.5%	-2.4%
3 Years	-19.1%	39.5%	5.6%
5 Years	-13.9%	58.1%	14.4%
10 Years	3.9%	192.3%	104.4%
Since May 2010	22.3%	292.2%	260.7%
Since May 2010 c.p.a.	1.5%	10.8%	10.1%

Returns in euro.   Source: Bloomberg, GillenMarkets.

In comparison, an investment in the European DGCFS provided a total return of 260.7% (with dividends reinvested), or 10.1% compound *per annum*. These returns are modestly behind those generated by the FTSE All-World Total Return Index in euro terms over the same timeframe.

In contrast with the US DGCFS, the European basket has not held up quite as well over the past two years. Since global equity markets peaked in November 2021, the European stocks in the theme have delivered a total return of -5.8%, compared to a -0.5% return from the FTSE All-World Total Return Index in euro terms over the same timeframe. This may reflect specific issues affecting European stocks, such as the war in Ukraine, the ECB's slow reaction to inflation in the Eurozone, and persistently high inflation in the UK.

2: EARNINGS RESILIENCE IS AT THE HEART OF THE THEME

Chart 3 highlights the earnings growth of both the US & European DGCFS since we introduced the theme in May 2010. The US & European DGCFS have similar globally diversified earnings bases. Both earnings series have been rebased to 100 at 28th May 2010.

Chart 3: US & European DGCFS: Earnings (rebased)

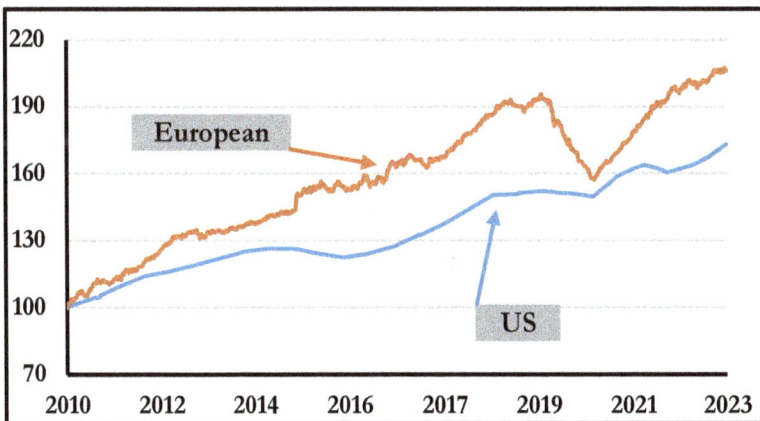

Source: Value Line, Annual Reports, GillenMarkets.

Since late May 2010, earnings growth for the US & European DGCFS have been 4.2% and 5.6% compound *per annum,* respectively. These returns are presented in euros and US dollars.

The earnings series diverged from May 2010, with earnings growth from the European franchises being significantly stronger than their US counterparts. It's possible that dollar strength from 2011 up until late 2015, and again in 2022, assisted the European DGCFS earnings series and, simultaneously, held back the international earnings of the US DGCFS. Earnings for the European DGCFS were also harder hit in 2020 than their US counterparts, reflecting a more pronounced impact of shutdowns on Heineken and Diageo and the more severe COVID-19 lockdowns in Europe compared to the US. Starting in mid-2021, we saw a significant recovery in the European DGCFS as lockdowns eased, and earnings are now 6% above the 2019 pre-COVID levels.

As you will see later in this report, the theme normally stands out for the resilience in earnings across these baskets of stocks. However, 2020-21 was a rare exception due to the impact of the shutdowns, which badly affected any company selling into the hospitality sector. In other words, 2020-21 period was (hopefully!) a rare exception as stocks of all colours, cyclical and defensive alike, were impacted.

Although earnings at the US & European DGCFS did decline during the pandemic, it is nonetheless worth noting that the fall in earnings was, in aggregate, much less severe than general industry. It is this durability of earnings and dividends that gives the theme bond-like characteristics. We will also note, later on, that the DGCFS have done an excellent job of raising prices to offset input-cost inflation, thus proving that this basket of stocks has earnings that are not just defensive during recessions, but also during inflationary periods.

At 1st September 2023, the eight US stocks making up the US DGCFS Theme were trading on an average price-to-earnings ratio of 22.9 and offered a starting dividend yield of 2.15%, while the six stocks making up the European DGCFS Theme were trading on an average price-to-earnings ratio of 18.5 and offered a starting dividend yield of 2.73% (*Table 4*).

Table 4: DGCFS Theme: Current Value & Dividend Statistics

Company	Sector	Share Price	P/E Ratio *	Div. Yield*
US Stocks:				
Brown Forman	Distillers	$66.74	32.7	1.26%
Coca-Cola	Non-alcoholic beverages	$59.31	22.5	3.02%
Colgate	Oral care, personal care, pet food	$73.27	23.1	2.67%
Const. Brands	Distillers	$259.48	22.0	1.37%
Kenvue	Consumer health products	$22.96	17.8	1.90%
McDonald's	Casual dining	$280.94	24.4	2.19%
Mondelēz Int'l	Snacks, sweets, chocolates	$69.69	21.4	2.29%
P & G	Household goods, personal care	$154.51	24.2	2.49%
Average PER & Yield			**22.9**	**2.15%**
European Stocks:				
Diageo	Distillers, brewers	£32.00	19.2	2.63%
Haleon	Oral care & healthcare	£3.20	18.2	1.66%
Heineken	Brewers	€89.56	17.9	2.06%
Nestlé	Snacks, personal care, pet food	105.46 CHF	21.2	2.92%
Reckitt	Health, hygiene, home care	£57.10	17.0	3.33%
Unilever	Food, personal & home care	£40.29	18.0	3.75%
Average PER & Yield			**18.5**	**2.73%**

* 2023 forecasts used.   Source: Bloomberg.

3: BUILDING A SUSTAINABLE & GROWING DIVIDEND STREAM

In May 2010, when we first introduced the theme, the risk-free US 10-year government bond offered a yield to maturity of 3.29%. At the same time, the US DGCFS in the theme offered a starting dividend yield of 3.33%.

Chart 4: US 10-Year Bond Yield v US DGCFS Dividend Yield

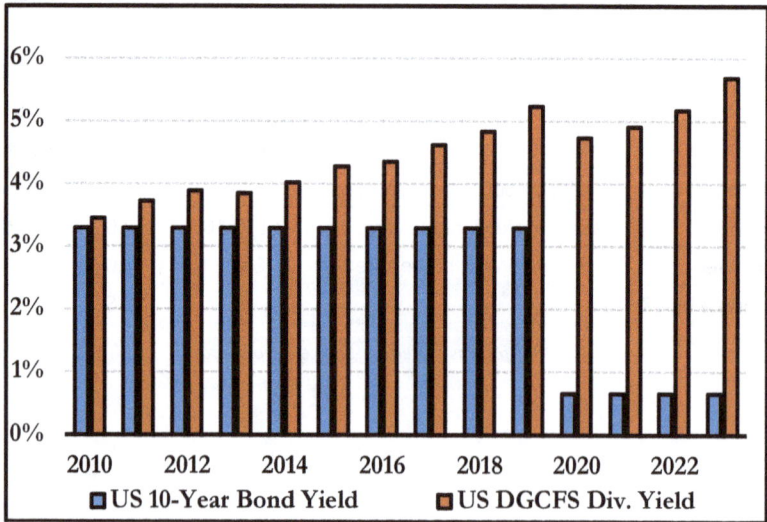

Source: Bloomberg, Annual Reports, Value Line.

The US 10-year bond purchased back in 2010 matured at end May 2020 and an investor who wanted no risk at that stage had to reinvest the proceeds into a new 10-year US government bond with a yield of just 0.65% for the next 10 years (with no prospect of growth in that yield).

In contrast, the dividend yield of the US DGCFS compared to the initial investment in May 2010 is now 5.69% and still growing as at 1st September 2023. (You will notice a slight dip in the yield in 2020: this is due to the removal of Kellogg and the introduction of Brown Forman, Clorox, and Constellation Brands – all of whose dividend yields were lower than Kellogg's at the time.)

For the European equivalents, the German 10-year government bond offered an annual yield to maturity of 2.68% at end May 2010. At that time, the basket of European DGCFS offered an initial dividend yield of 2.65%.

Chart 5: German 10-Year Bond Yield v European DGCFS Dividend Yield

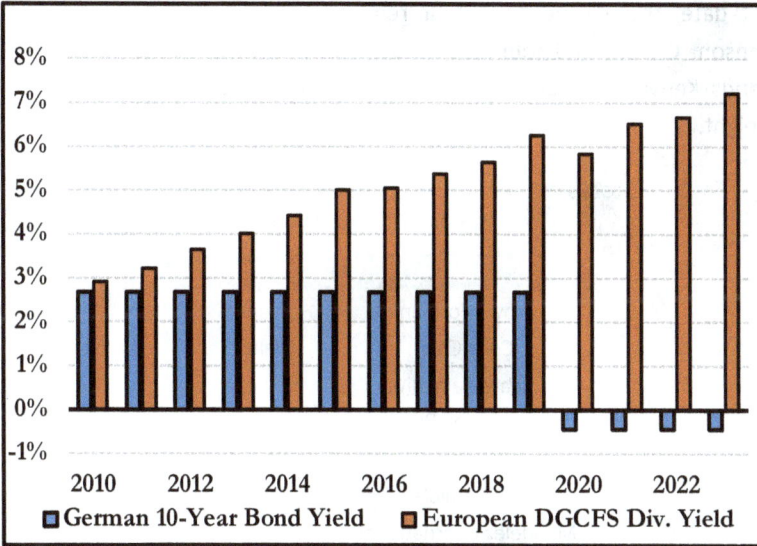

Source: Bloomberg, Annual Reports.

The German 10-year bond that was purchased at end May 2010 matured in late May 2020 and an investor had to reinvest the proceeds into a German 10-year bond offering a negative yield of -0.45%, if they wanted to continue to take no risk for the next 10 years. Again, there is no prospect of growth in this yield, just an assured annual loss.

In contrast, at 1st September 2023 the European DGCFS were providing a dividend yield of 7.2% on the initial investment in May 2010, and the dividend yield is likely to continue to grow.

4: THE THEME IN MORE DETAIL

Table 5 shows the stocks currently in the US and European baskets. The US basket was introduced in May 2010, and had eight stocks at the time. Since that date, there have been four removals (Walmart, Kellogg, Johnson & Johnson, Clorox) and four additions (Brown Forman, Clorox, Constellation Brands, Kenvue) so that the total number of stocks in the US basket still stands at eight.

Table 5: Stocks in the US & European Defensive Global Consumer Franchise Stocks Theme

US	European
Brown Forman	Diageo
Coca-Cola	Haleon
Colgate-Palmolive	Heineken
Constellation Brands	Nestlé
Kenvue	Reckitt
McDonald's	Unilever
Mondelēz International	
Procter & Gamble	

The European equivalents of Diageo, Heineken, Nestlé, Reckitt, and Unilever were added to the theme at various dates between 2011 and 2015. Henkel and Kerry have been removed as we have decided they do not fit the theme (Henkel's revenues can be cyclical and Kerry, while it sells to consumer franchises, is not itself a consumer franchise). We added Haleon in 2023 when it split off from GSK.

This makes for eight US and six European companies, or 14 in all. The common characteristics of the companies are that they are all global operators with demand resilience and either some pricing power or a low-cost advantage (such as McDonald's).

The theme provides investors with a way to gain low-risk access to the returns available from equity markets. Our belief is that buying into companies with global manufacturing and distribution, demand resilience, low financial risk, strong brands, and/or a low-cost competitive advantage should provide investors with a diversified basket of companies capable of delivering a consistent and growing earnings stream, but, critically, with defensiveness in periods of turbulence or recession, and the ability to pass on rising input costs in inflationary periods. The nature of these brands is that they are daily essentials or small luxuries that consumers value highly – and for which there is no replacement in their mind.

Earnings Power Over the Long Term

The US Basket

Over the long-term the DGCFS have, collectively, a highly impressive record of growth and a much lower risk profile compared to mainstream equities.

Chart 6 displays the earnings growth record of the US DGCFS from the start of 1989 to 1st September 2023 – a period of nearly 35 years. Stocks which have been added or removed are included/excluded from the date of their inclusion/ removal.

Over this period, the US DGCFS have grown their collective earnings by 8.4% compound *per annum* (in dollar terms). In contrast, earnings growth generated by the 500 companies making up the S&P 500 Index has, on average, been a lower 6.2% compound *per annum* over the same period.

Earnings growth has also been more erratic for the S&P 500, as highlighted in *Chart 6*. For the stock market as a whole, corporate earnings decline during recessions. Not generally so, apparently, for the DGCFS and therein lies the attraction of these types of companies. The year 2020, of course, was a rare exception to this general rule. Even then, however, the decline in the US DGCFS was much less severe than was the case for overall equities.

Chart 6: Earnings Growth; US DGCFS v S&P 500 (1989-2023)

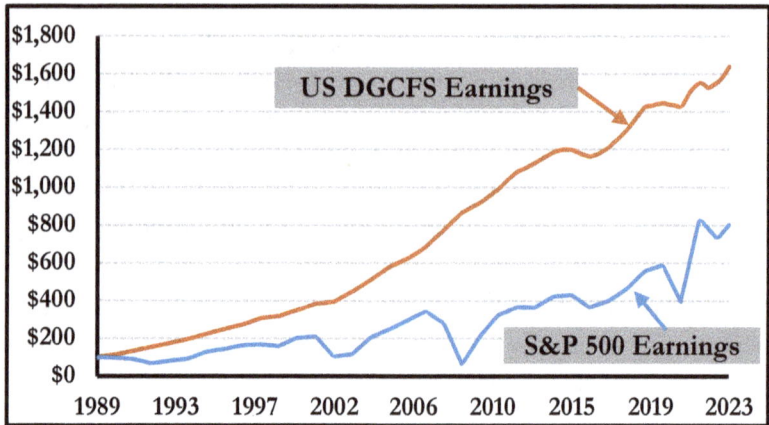

Source: Value Line, S&P Dow Jones Indices.

In aggregate, over this same 35-year period, the US DGCFS have registered only two periods of negative earnings growth – and this despite four recessions in the developed world (1991, 2001-02, 2007-09, 2020-21).

The US DGCFS endured a modest 3.6% decline in earnings between 2014 and 2016. Dollar strength was a feature at that time, and this meant lower earnings when translating overseas earnings back to dollars during that period. However, this same basket of US DGCFS dealt more easily with dollar strength back in the 1995 to 2001 period. So, exchange rate movements alone were unlikely to be the reason for the earnings dip in the 2014-16 period. More likely, pressure from changing consumer preferences (looking for healthier options, less processed foods, lower sugar, etc.) and the fragmentation of the retail channel, particularly with the growth of online retail sales, has provided real challenges for some of the companies in the theme. That said, earnings growth for the US stocks in the theme recovered thereafter and went on to new peaks.

Earnings for the 2020-21 period declined 1.6%, which is particularly remarkable considering that the S&P 500's earnings declined 32.4% over the same period.

Table 6 outlines the earnings and price growth statistics over the 13-year period for S&P 500 and the US DGCFS.

Table 6: US DGCFS: Growth Statistics (*c.p.a.*) (May 2010 to September 2023)

	Total Returns	Earnings
US DGCFS	10.1%	4.2%
S&P 500 Index	13.5%	8.8%

Source: Value Line, S&P Dow Jones Indices.

Over this period, earnings growth for the eight US DGCFS grew 4.2% compound *per annum* compared to 8.8% compound *per annum* for the S&P 500 Index earnings (all in dollar terms).

The strong performance of the S&P 500 over this period reflects, in part, a strong recovery from the 2008-09 financial crisis when earnings were at a low. The US corporate tax rate was also lowered in 2018, disproportionately benefitting the S&P 500 Index, which has a higher proportion of earnings in the US than the more internationally focused US DGCFS. In addition, faster earnings growth in the technology sector is a structural trend and continues to benefit the S&P 500 Index stocks over the DGCFS.

It is worth remembering that the theme was not introduced as a way to generate above-average earnings growth. Indeed, many of the stocks in the theme are behemoths operating in mature markets – we should expect them to grow at low-to-mid-single-digit rates. The point of the theme is to identify and invest in stocks that have resilient earnings which can grow their revenue, earnings, and dividends such that investors can earn the returns available from equities over time (and above government bonds) while taking on less risk than general equities.

The list of stocks in the US basket is by no means exhaustive. It's important to say that not all of these US DGCFS grew earnings every year. For example, McDonald's encountered problems in the 1998 to 2003 period where earnings declined, and the business underwent significant structural changes. And, more recently, Colgate has been undergoing restructurings to counter changing consumer preferences and the pressure from online sales. But, in aggregate, their earnings have been very resilient.

Reflecting the lower level of earnings growth, the US DGCFS have delivered total returns (capital growth plus dividends reinvested) of 10.1% compound *per annum* since May 2010, lower than for the S&P 500 Index which delivered a 13.5% compound *per annum* return over this same period.

The European Basket

If we look to Europe, we see the same pattern of earnings resilience. The European DGCFS are Diageo, Heineken, Haleon, Nestlé, Reckitt, and Unilever. Again, this is by no means an exhaustive list, but it does cover a diverse group of defensive consumer companies providing a variety of products and services.

For the US basket, we are fortunate to have access to the Value Line database, which has allowed our records to extend back to the late 1980s.

For the European equivalents, we have not been so fortunate and the best we have been able to achieve has been to take our data back to late 1999 (for all stocks bar Heineken).

Chart 7: European DGCFS: Earnings Growth (2000-2023) (rebased to 100)

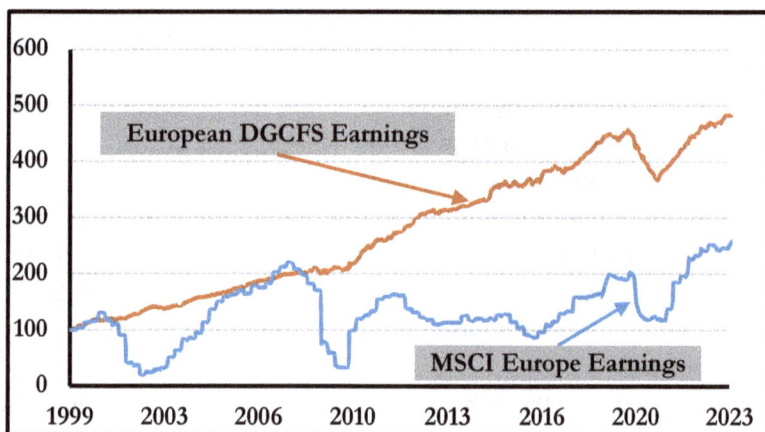

Source: Bloomberg, Annual Reports.

Chart 7 highlights the earnings growth of these companies from late 1999 to September 2023 and again highlights the uninterrupted earnings progress from these European DGCFS as a group. The exception, of course, has been 2020 (for reasons previously discussed).

Over the 23-year period from late 1999 to September 2023, these European DGCFS have grown their collective earnings by 6.9% compound *per annum* (in euro terms). Over the same period, earnings for the MSCI Europe Index grew by 3.9% compound *per annum*.

Table 7 outlines the earnings growth statistics over the shorter 13-year period that the theme has been running from May 2010 to September 2023.

Table 7: European DGCFS: Growth Statistics (*c.p.a.*)
(May 2010 to September 2023)

	Total Returns	Earnings
European DGCFS	10.1%	5.6%
MSCI Europe Index	8.1%	6.0%

Source: Bloomberg, Annual Reports.

Over this 13-year period, earnings growth for the European DGCFS grew 5.6% compound *per annum*, compared to 6.0% compound *per annum* for the MSCI Europe Index earnings (in euro terms). Earnings growth for the European index has accelerated of late, reflecting a strong recovery from the impact of the COVID-19 lockdowns. Prior to this, earnings growth had been volatile, hampered by a series of factors, including a higher reliance on more cyclical sectors such as oil and banking, and lower exposure to technology stocks.

The European DGCFS have delivered total returns of 10.1% compound *per annum* since May 2010 (capital growth plus dividends reinvested), in excess of the MSCI Europe Index which delivered an 8.1% compound *per annum* return over this same period (again in euro terms).

Slower Earnings Growth Today

As *Table 8* highlights, earnings growth in the 2010 decade (2010-2019 inclusive) was lower than in the previous two decades. For large, mature businesses, this is unsurprising – double-digit growth rates are unlikely to continue forever. Global GDP growth since the start of the 2010s was also slower than in previous decades. That said, we have always promoted the theme on the basis of earnings growth being sustained at a lower rate of *circa*

3% to 5%, and we don't require double-digit earnings growth rates for the theme to serve an investor's needs.

Table 8: Earnings Growth: US & European DGCFS

	US DGCFS ($)	European DGCFS (€)
1990s	11.9%	n/a
2000s	10.2%	8.2%
2010s	4.6%	7.5%
2020s	3.6%	1.8%

Source: Value Line, Annual Reports.

Explaining the Defensive / Growth Characteristics

Building a go-to brand can take years and when you have a recognised brand you often have pricing power, and this allows such companies to pass on cost increases more easily.

Of the 14 stocks in our US & European DGCFS Theme, all have leading brands with number one positions in various sectors – like Coca-Cola in non-alcoholic drinks, Diageo (Guinness, Johnny Walker whisky), Heineken (speaks for itself), Mondelēz (Cadbury), Unilever (Dove, Magnum), Reckitt (Dettol, Durex, Finish) and so on. Over the years this has tended to afford such companies some pricing power.

Most of these products are consumed regularly by customers and, with low ticket prices, demand tends to be very stable, even in recessionary conditions. It's the big not-necessary-now products like cars, homes, expensive holidays, etc., that get shelved in tougher economic times.

Further, many of these products deal with highly personal necessities – such as oral, health, and personal care – and consumers are often reluctant to switch to other brands or generic alternatives as trust has been built up in their preferred brand.

McDonald's offering is slightly different – it's a very competitive low-cost, convenient food service offering delivered reliably worldwide.

These characteristics generally lead to consistent earnings growth, as well as delivering above-average returns on capital for these businesses. The resultant strong cash flows can be invested in more marketing and expansion and new product initiatives which drives growth and supports the brands further. If growth opportunities dry up, then excess cash flows can go to support stronger dividend growth and/or share buy-backs.

For decades, these characteristics have meant that such companies carried very low levels of business risk compared to general equities.

Burnishing The Inflation-Busting Credentials

We have been saying, ever since the launch of the theme, that these companies' brands give them significant pricing power. But, this has never been put to a true test! Inflation over the period from 2010-2021 was quite moderate. However, the past 18 months have, especially in the developed world, seen a significant resurgence of inflation following this period of little to no inflation. For example, inflation in 2022 was 8.0% in the US while inflation reached 9.2% in the EU.

This provided ample opportunity for these companies to prove that they can raise prices without, as Warren Buffett says, having "a prayer session before raising the price by a tenth of a cent."

The implication of inflation for companies is rising costs – be it labour, transportation, raw materials, etc. In turn, companies must push through price increases for their products and services in an effort to offset these higher costs. But not all businesses are made equal – some find it easier than others to push through higher prices. The key question for many management teams is: how much can we raise prices for our customers without wrecking our businesses?

The key to being able to raise prices without losing customers is to offer a product or service that is irreplaceable in customers' minds – perhaps an everyday essential item, or a small luxury that customers are unwilling to cut back on. These, in effect, describe very well the products sold by our basket of DGCFS. Is there really any substitute for Heineken, Guinness (Diageo), Sensodyne (Haleon), Nurofen (Reckitt), Dairy Milk (Mondelēz), Coca-Cola, Jack Daniels (Brown Forman), or Ariel (Procter & Gamble)?

Of course, no moat is perfect – these companies must compete for customers' dollars both with similar branded products and generic alternatives. Nonetheless, clever marketing and an emphasis on quality products has placed these brands high in customers' esteem. This preferred status gives these companies defensiveness in recession, and the ability to raise prices without impacting business. In other words, these companies have strong pricing power, as evidenced by *Table 9*.

Table 9: DGCFS Theme: Dealing with Inflation

| | 2022 | | 6 Months to June 2023 | |
	Price	Volume	Price	Volume
US Stocks:				
Brown Forman**	8.0%	9.0%	3.0%	8.0%
Coca-Cola	11.0%	5.0%	10.5%	1.0%
Colgate	9.5%	-2.5%	11.5%	-2.5%
Constellation Brands¥	7.2%	0.3%	4.4%	3.6%
Kenvue	-	-	9.0%	0.4%
Mondelēz	9.6%	2.7%	16.0%	1.6%
Procter & Gamble	8.0%	-1.8%	8.5%	-2.0%
Average	**9.4%**	**2.5%**	**9.2%**	**0.1%**
European Stocks:				
Diageo*	11.0%	10.3%	7.3%	-0.8%
Haleon	4.3%	4.7%	7.5%	2.9%
Heineken	14.8%	6.4%	12.7%	-5.6%
Nestlé	8.2%	0.1%	9.5%	-0.8%
Reckitt	9.8%	-2.2%	10.4%	-4.4%
Unilever	11.3%	-2.1%	9.4%	-0.3%

* Figures for Diageo are for FY 2022 (end June) and FY 2023.

** Figures for Brown Forman are for FY 2022 (end April) and FY 2023.

¥ Figures for Constellation are for FY 2022 (end February) and FY 2023.

Source: Annual & Interim Reports.

On average, the companies in the theme have pushed through price increases by an average of 9.4% in 2022, and a further 9.2% in the first half of 2023. These prices have been in line with, or even ahead of, inflation in the developed world. Even better, these price increases have been achieved without much impact on average volumes.

The table provides strong supporting evidence for the idea that these companies' revenues and earnings are resilient, not just to recessions, but to inflationary periods, too!

Risks from the Internet Are Real

The Internet is a massively disruptive force and is changing many traditional industries, introducing both new threats and new opportunities.

Brands and companies which were previously thought to have impenetrable moats have suddenly found themselves flat-footed and out-competed by small start-ups with not much capital but plenty of Internet savvy. Gillette (part of Procter & Gamble), for example, lost market share in its razors business to two Internet start-ups.

Social media is changing consumer buying habits and weakening brand power, and one must be alive to such risks. New tools, such as digital marketing, e-commerce, and direct-to-consumer distribution all need to be mastered in order to continue to thrive.

However, delivering value to the customer is key to the strength and durability of a competitive advantage. Brand recognition, distribution advantages, cost advantages make a lasting difference, if the customer is getting a good deal.

It's hard to see any real threats from the Internet for Coca-Cola's main carbonated drinks brands or for Diageo's major whisky and alcoholic beverage brands. Similarly, we see little threat from the Internet to Heineken's beer brand or Nestlé's food and beverages offerings. McDonald's has been a beneficiary of the Internet as the group is improving customer convenience with new online ordering and payment options.

All the giant global consumer franchise stocks have their competitive pressures whether that is from changing consumer preferences, regulatory pressures or new entrants with innovative offerings.

But companies with strong brands or low-cost competitive offerings and entrenched positions should be able to respond to changing consumer preferences and other competitive threats through new product developments, especially given the immense global distribution power and strong finances that they tend to have at their disposal. They may no longer be growing fast, but they are hard to move.

In recent years, the DGCFS have made decent strides to increase their online presence. *Table 10* highlights the progress made by several of the companies in the theme in terms of online revenues over the past few years – over the past several years, sales from online channels have increased three to four times for these companies (albeit from low levels).

Table 10: E-commerce Revenues as a % of Overall Company Revenues

	Colgate	Nestlé	P&G	RB	Unilever
2016	-	4.9%	6.0%	~5.0%	3.5%
2017	-	6.2%	7.0%	6.0%	3.9%
2018	5.0%	7.4%	8.0%	7.0%	5.0%
2019	6.0%	8.5%	10.0%	9.0%	6.0%
2020	9.0%	12.8%	14.0%	10.0%	9.0%
2021	13.0%	14.3%	14.0%	12.0%	13.0%
2022	14.0%	15.8%	17.0%	13.0%	15.0%

Source: Annual Reports.

Our point is that we need to be alive to fresh risks, but also recognise that these companies normally have the wherewithal to respond to new competitive threats and changing trends.

5: BALANCE SHEETS & CAPITAL ALLOCATION

Capital Allocation – Benefitting Shareholders

Share Buybacks

A common trend for companies in the DGCFS theme has been a significant increase in share buybacks over the last decade. Ongoing share buybacks provide an additional boost to earnings and cash flows per share over time and, in our view, are a sensible deployment of cashflow if capital expenditure projects or acquisitions cannot fully deploy a company's cash flows.

However, share buybacks come with *caveats*:

- It is important that shares are being bought back at or below intrinsic value; and

- Buybacks should benefit shareholders with a reduction in shares outstanding rather than offset shares issued as part of a company's stock-based compensation plan.

Chart 8 highlights the annual aggregate value of share buybacks for seven of the US companies[1] in the theme (**blue** bar, left-hand axis). Buybacks have been adjusted for shares issued under stock-based compensation plans. The chart also shows share buybacks as a percentage of average market cap (orange line, right-hand axis).

In the 10-year period from the end of 2012 to end 2022, these seven companies have returned a total of $110.2 billion to shareholders in the form of share buybacks – with the significant amount of share buybacks in 2016 reflecting large buyback programmes from McDonald's and Procter & Gamble.

---

[1] Brown Forman, Coca-Cola, Colgate-Palmolive, Constellation Brands, McDonald's, Mondelēz International and Procter & Gamble. Kenvue is a newly-formed company and thus excluded.

For Colgate, McDonald's, Mondelēz and Procter & Gamble, buybacks have been a feature of capital allocation on an annual basis.

Chart 8: US DGCFS: Share Buybacks ($bn) as % of Average Market Capitalisation

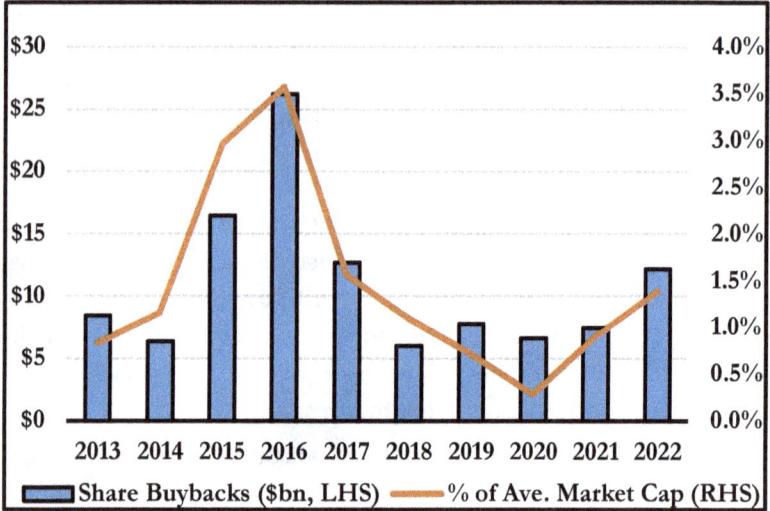

Source: Annual Reports, Bloomberg, GillenMarkets.

As the chart also highlights, in 2015 and 2016 share buybacks represented 3.0% and 3.6%, respectively, of the average market capitalisation of these companies. This figure dropped to just 0.3% during the COVID-19 pandemic while buybacks have ranged between 0.7% and 1.6% of average market value for the remaining years.

Table 11: US DGCFS: Total Change in Shares Outstanding (2012-2022)

	Brown Forman	Coca-Cola	Colgate	Const. Brands	McDonald's	Mondelēz	P&G
Change	-10.3%	-2.8%	-11.3%	-3.5%	-27.1%	-23.2%	-13.9%

Source: Annual Reports.

Overall, the basket of US companies in the theme have allocated a significant amount of capital to share buybacks over the last decade and while stock issuance for compensation plans has offset this somewhat, we have seen meaningful reductions in shares outstanding over this period – with notable reductions in shares outstanding for Brown Forman, Colgate, McDonald's, Mondelēz, and Procter & Gamble.

Similarly, ***Chart 9*** presents the same information for the six European companies in the theme.

Chart 9: European DGCFS: Share Buybacks (€bn) as % of Average Market Capitalisation

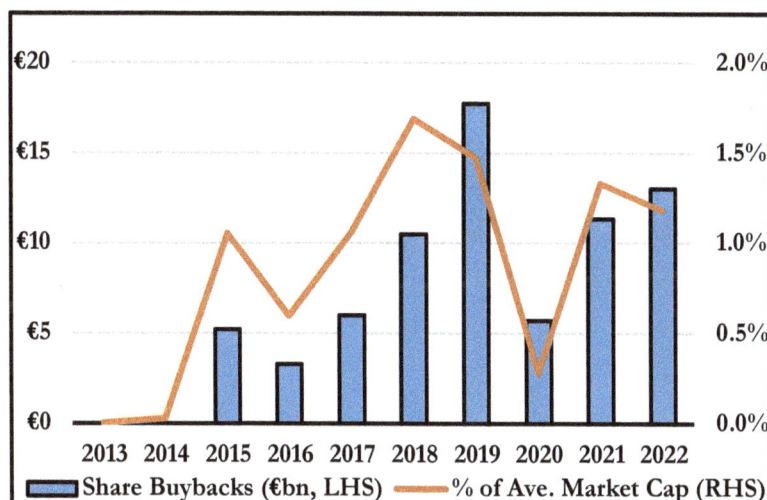

Source: Annual Reports, Bloomberg, GillenMarkets.

Over the period from end 2012 to 2022, the total value of share buybacks has equalled €72.8 billion with little to no share buybacks in 2013 and 2014.

Since 2015, share buybacks as a percentage of average market capitalisation has ranged from 0.6% to 1.7% with the exception of 2020 of just 0.3% as companies pared back spending during the COVID-19 pandemic.

Table 12: European DGCFS: Total Change in Shares Outstanding (2012 - 2022)

	Diageo	Heineken	Nestlé	Reckitt	Unilever
Change	-10.7%	0.0%	-16.3%	-0.5%	-10.6%

We do not include Haleon as it was only formed in July 2022

Source: Annual Reports.

Within the European basket, share buybacks have been concentrated in Diageo, Nestlé and Unilever with buybacks not being a significant feature of Heineken's and Reckitt's capital allocation over the last decade. Nonetheless, **Table 12** shows a reduction by the European DGCFS in the number of shares in issue by over 10% over the last decade.

Dividends

Steady and (modestly) growing dividends is a fundamental characteristic of the DGCFS and a key element of shareholders' returns. **Table 13** summarises dividend payments for both the US and the European companies in the theme for the 10-year period between 2013 and 2022.

Table 13: Dividends

	US $bn	Europe €bn
2013	17.6	11.7
2014	18.8	12.5
2015	19.5	14.0
2016	20.1	14.0
2017	20.3	14.4
2018	21.2	14.5
2019	22.3	15.2
2020	23.8	15.6
2021	24.4	17.2
2022	25.4	19.7
Total	$213.4	€148.7

Source: Annual Reports.

For the seven US companies in the Theme (excluding Kenvue, as it is a new company), total dividend payments over the last 10 years have amounted to $213.4 billion. Part of the growth in dividend income over the past 10 years has come from a higher payout ratio, meaning that a greater proportion of earnings has been dedicated to dividend payments. In 2013, the dividend payout ratio for these companies was 41%, and this increased to 54% in 2022.

Combined with the $110.2 billion of share buybacks outlined in the previous section, the US companies have returned a total of $323.7 billion to shareholders over the last decade. This compares to an aggregate market value of $579.0 billion for these companies 10 years ago, and $422.3 billion of aggregate operating cash flows over 10 years. In other words, these companies have returned 56% of their starting market cap to shareholders in a decade, and 76% of total operating cash flows.

For the European equivalents, the six companies in the theme have returned a total of €148.7 billion to shareholders through dividends since 2013. The dividend payout ratio has remained constant at c. 53% for the European DGCFS.

Combined with the €72.8 billion of share buybacks, the European DGCFS have returned a total of €221.5 billion to shareholders over the last decade. This compares to an aggregate market value of €392.5 billion and €296.7 billion of aggregate operating cash flows, such that the European companies have also returned 56% of their starting market value and 75% of their total cash flow to shareholders over the past decade.

The companies in the theme are large and operate in mature markets so large growth capital expenditure projects and/or major acquisition opportunities are rare. It makes sense, then, to see large amounts of capital being returned to shareholders.

Overall, on balance, it appears clear to us that these companies' Boards of Directors are allocating capital efficiently, making sure to return surplus (unneeded) cash flows to shareholders.

30   ICONIC CONSUMER BRANDS FOR MORE DEFENSIVE, LOWER-RISK INVESTING

Debt Helping to Fund Share Buybacks

While it is true that mature companies such as these DGCFS don't have as many opportunities to re-invest capital as younger companies, their requirement for capital is not zero.

In other words, these companies should retain *some* operating cash flows to fund maintenance and strategic capital expenditures, as well as fund mergers & acquisitions.

Table 14 highlights that the gearing (indebtedness) ratios for the franchises have increased over the past decade. This allows us to infer that, after adjusting for re-investment of cash flows in the business, the companies have chosen to return more cash to shareholders than has been generated over the past 10 years – and the excess has been funded by taking out debt.

Table 14: DGCFS Theme: Finances – Net Debt / OCF

	2013	Today
European Stocks:		
Diageo	4.3x	5.1x
Heineken	4.6x	3.0x
Nestlé	1.2x	4.1x
Reckitt	1.3x	2.8x
Unilever	1.2x	3.3x
Average	2.5x	3.7x
US Stocks:		
Brown Forman	1.5x	4.0x
Coca-Cola	1.5x	2.5x
Colgate	1.4x	3.1x
Constellation Brands	5.3x	4.5x
McDonalds	1.6x	4.5x
Mondelēz	3.8x	5.4x
P&G	1.7x	1.6x
Average	2.4x	3.6x

Source: Annual Reports.

Boards and management have, in effect, taken advantage of a period of ultra-low interest rates to fund buyback programmes with long-term debt fixed at low rates of interest.

As we can see from *Table 14*, net debt was 2.5 times operating cash flow, on average, for the European companies in 2013. Today, this has risen to 3.7 times cash flows.

And the story is similar for the basket of US companies – with net debt rising from 2.4 times operating cash flows in 2013 to 3.6 times today.

In aggregate, these companies have increased their debt loads significantly, and at least part of the explanation for this lies in the large amount of capital returned *via* share buybacks.

We believe, however, that these companies cannot continue to increase their debt burdens indefinitely in order to fund returns to shareholders. With balance sheets now appearing close to "fully loaded" in our view, we expect that the pace of share buybacks is likely to taper down in the future.

A falling share count must, just by pure mechanics, increase earnings on a per-share basis because of a lower denominator. Going forward, we expect that this tailwind to per-share earnings growth is likely to have less effect. Overall, however, we continue to view financial risks as low. As a reminder, we define financial risk as:

> The risk of inappropriate financing and debt levels, which exposes the company to failure and investors to a potential total loss.

We believe this has not changed despite the recent rise in debt loads. Cash flows are defensive, predictable, and inflation-resistant. The majority of debt taken on is at fixed rates and is long-term in nature. The companies are all assigned investment grade ratings, thus giving easy access to capital markets. So, we see current debt levels as manageable.

6: VALUATION RISKS

Far Better Value than Government Bonds – Still?

The first comparison we make when valuing the US & European DGCFS is with the respective 10-year government bonds, which offer a risk-free fixed-income stream, but with no opportunity for growth in that income stream over the life of the bond.

The reliability of earnings at the DGCFS and their ability to grow earnings consistently appear to offer investors a low-risk income (earnings) stream and one that grows over time. Thus, we feel that the income stream from the US & European DGCFS can be compared to the income available from 10-year government bonds in the US and Europe.

Chart 10: US DGCFS Earnings Yield v US 10-Year Bond Yields (1989-2023)

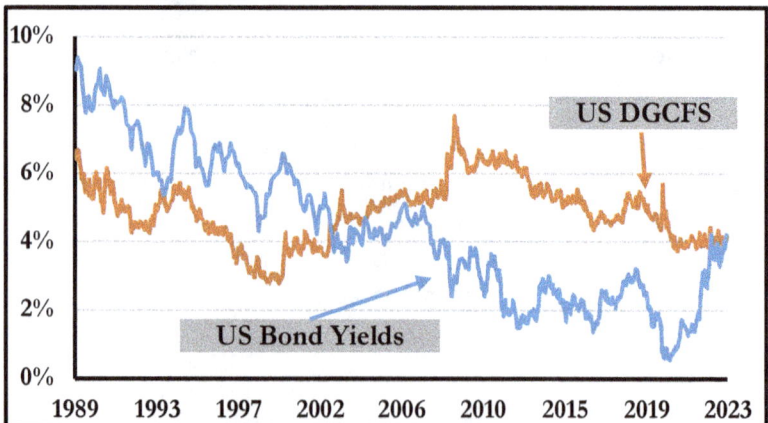

Source: Bloomberg, Value Line, GillenMarkets.

Chart 10 displays the earnings yield on the US DGCFS (blue line) compared to the yield on a US 10-year government bond (orange line). An earnings yield simply tells you how much earnings you are getting for every dollar that you invest in a stock.

For example, if Coca-Cola is expected to earn $2.64 a share in 2023 and you buy the shares today at *circa* $59, you are buying an earnings yield of 4.5% ($2.64 / $59 * 100 = 4.5%).

Currently, the average earnings yield for the eight US DGCFS is 4.19%, and this compares to a yield of 4.19% from the US 10-year Government bond.

The earnings yield on the US DGCFS has been consistently declining since we initiated the theme in 2010, falling from 6.55% in May 2010 to the 4.19% we see today. In other words, investors have been willing to pay higher prices for this basket of stocks, likely reflecting falling interest rates in the US and the (rising) bull market over the period in question. This fall in the earnings yield explains a large proportion of the difference in earnings growth for the US basket (+4.2% annually since May 2010) *versus* the total returns earned by investors in these stocks (+10.1% annually).

Since the initiation of the theme in May 2010, the average earnings yield for the US basket of stocks was 5.19%. The average US 10-year bond yield was 2.13%. So, without even accounting for earnings growth from the companies, this basket of stocks offered a reasonable risk premium over risk-free government bonds – making our investment case reasonably simple!

Over the past 18 months, however, we have seen interest rates in the US begin to rise. From a low point of 0.53% in 2020, the US 10-year bond yield has increased to 4.19% currently. At the same time, the earnings yield for the US basket of stocks has remained stable at *c.* 4%, reflecting investors' appreciation of these companies' defensive and inflation-resistant earnings in a volatile period.

This means that the risk premium between the two has narrowed and the value on offer, *relative* to government bonds, has decreased. However, equities are capable of growing their revenues and earnings over time, which adds to the total returns earned by shareholders.

With a starting dividend yield of 2.15% and earnings growth of perhaps 3% to 5% annually from here (in line with the long-term average), these stocks offer annualised total returns of 5% to 7% for long-term investors – still a decent risk premium over the risk-free alternative, at least at the higher end of the earnings growth projections.

And it's no different for the European equivalents. With rising interest rates in Europe, the gap between the earnings yield and the risk-free government bond yield (an average of German and UK 10-year bonds) has narrowed.

However, unlike the US, the gap between the two is still reasonably wide. **Chart 11** highlights that the current average earnings yield available from the European DGCFS is 5.39%. The average 10-year bond yield is 3.49%, so the gap between the two is *c.* 1.9%. The reason for the difference between the European and US stocks is explained both by a lower valuation applied by the market to the European DGCFS, and lower interest rates in continental Europe compared to the US.

Chart 11: European DGCFS Earnings Yield v US 10-Year Bond Yields (1999-2023)

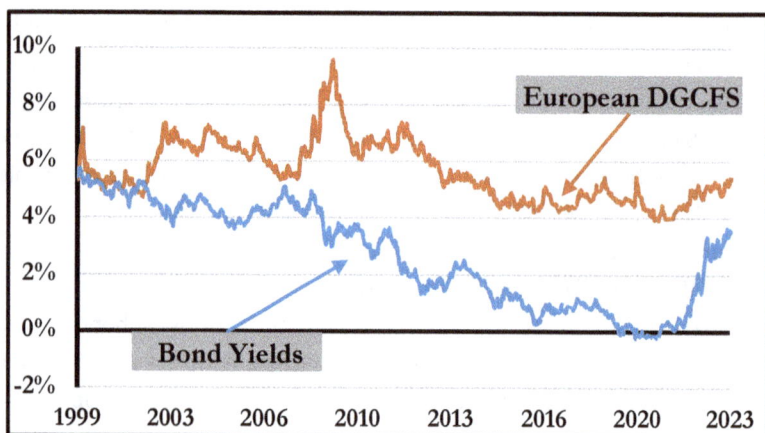

Source: Bloomberg, Annual Reports, GillenMarkets.

Similar to the US stocks, the earnings yield for the European DGCFS has been falling over time, from 6.57% at the initiation of the theme in May 2010 to 5.4% currently (although up from a low of 4% in 2020). This goes some way to explaining the difference between earnings growth (5.6% annualised since May 2010) and total returns earned by investors in these companies (10.1% annualised).

While the gap between the earnings yield and the 10-year government bond yield has narrowed over time, it is still reasonably substantial at 1.9%. The

European DGCFS offer an initial dividend yield of 2.73%. Combined with earnings growth of perhaps 3% to 5% annually from here, the potential for 6% to 8% total annualised returns from here (over the long-term) appears entirely plausible – which would represent a decent risk premium over the risk-free alternative.

Valuation Relative to History

Next, we will compare what investors have been willing historically to pay for each dollar of earnings for our basket of US DGCFS.

Chart 12 highlights that, since 1989, investors have on average been willing to pay a price-to-earnings ratio of 20.5 for the historic earnings of the US DGCFS. Today, investors are paying 23.9 times historic earnings for these stocks, which is above the historical average. (This figure differs from what is shown in **Table 4**, as here we use a weighted average of historic and forecast next-year earnings.)

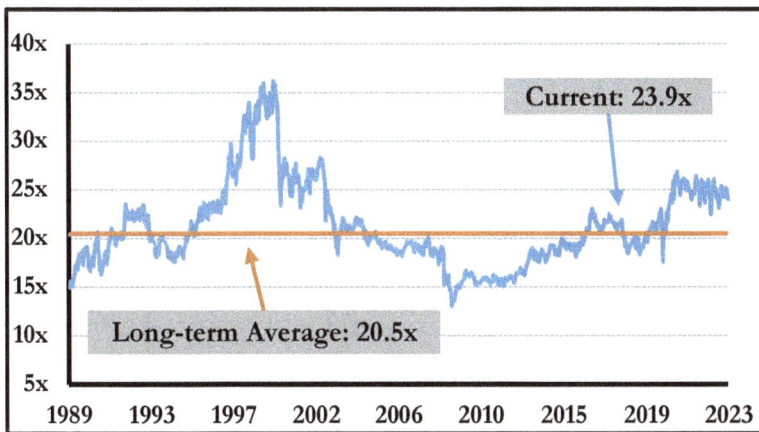

Chart 12: US DGCFS: Price-to-earnings Ratio

Source: Bloomberg, Value Line, GillenMarkets.

The picture is slightly different for the European consumer franchises. As **Chart 13** highlights, the average price-to-earnings ratio for the seven European stocks is 18.6 at present and below the US equivalents. (Again, this figure differs from **Table 5** due to our use of a weighted average of historic and forecast next-year earnings.)

Chart 13: European DGCFS: Price-to-earnings Ratio

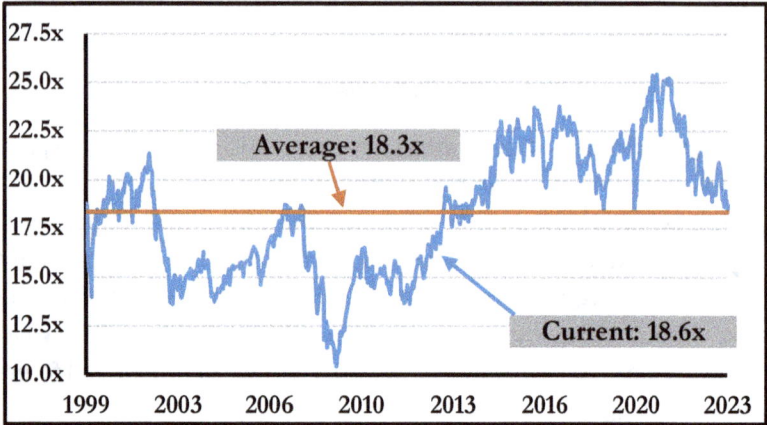

Source: Bloomberg, Annual Reports, GillenMarkets.

The price-to-earnings ratio for the European DGCFS has contracted significantly over the past two years, reflecting in the main a strong recovery in Diageo's and Heineken's earnings, both of which were heavily impacted in the COVID-19 lockdowns.

Still Better Value than the Market?

Our final method of comparison is to look at what investors are willing to pay for the US & European DGCFS *versus* what they are willing to pay for equities generally.

For 2023, S&P 500 Index earnings are expected to reach *c.* $200 an index share (a new all-time high, slightly above the previous 2021 peak of $198). At the time of writing, the S&P 500 index is trading at $4,516 and is, therefore, trading on 22.6 times 2023 expected earnings.

The US DGCFS are trading on a forecast 2023 price-to-earnings ratio of 23.9, meaning that they are trading slightly above the market.

For the European basket, the average price-to-earnings ratio is 18.6, which compares to 12.9 for the MSCI Europe Index.

Summing Up the Valuation Risks

In concluding on the valuation risks in the theme, we find ourselves compelled to talk separately about the US & European DGCFS.

For the US, sharply rising interest rates means that the gap between the earnings yield and the US 10-year government bond yield is now zero. Further, the US basket is trading at a premium to its own valuation history, and in line with the valuation of the S&P 500.

In other words, we must conclude that valuations for the US basket are, at least, at fair value. They are certainly not at bargain basement prices! However, an investment in these US companies still holds significant attractions: world-class brands; defensive, predictable revenues and earnings; and an element of inflation protection, as evidenced by the ability to push through price increases over the past 18 months.

Our estimated total return of 5% to 7% annually represents a modest-to-decent risk premium over the risk-free 10-year government bond, but we caution that the 10% annualised returns (earned since initiation of the theme in May 2010) are unlikely to be repeated, given the mature nature of the businesses and thus the low likelihood of generating high-single-digit earnings growth from here. Any further rises in interest rates are also likely to challenge the valuations of the DGCFS, too.

For Europe, the valuation risks appear more modest. The gap between the earnings yield and the 10-year government bond yield is 1.9% and valuations are in line with the long-term average. While valuations are higher than the MSCI Europe Index, this likely reflects depressed valuations in Europe rather than overvaluation for the basket.

Our estimated total return of 5% to 8% continues to represent a good risk premium over risk-free 10-year government bonds, and investors also benefit from all of the attractions already mentioned: world-class brands; defensive, predictable revenues and earnings; and an element of inflation protection.

CONCLUDING REMARKS

A Good Alternative to Government Bonds

The DGCFS won't always match the returns from general equities. They are, on average, very large companies, and in many cases somewhat mature. But, in our view, they carry less risk than general equities and their bond-like characteristics, as a basket of companies, make them a suitable alternative to government bonds, although as we have noted, the recent rise in government bond yields has made long-dated government bonds a more credible alternative over the past 18 months (particularly in the US).

Clearly, share prices of all listed companies are volatile whereas, with developed world government bonds, your capital is not at risk so long as you hold to maturity. That said, volatility is less important for the medium- and long-term investor, as earnings growth (inflation-protected, in this case!) acts as a natural upwards pull for companies' share prices.

We can't be sure which companies will do better than average over time, in which case diversification is important. Kellogg, for example, was a notable laggard over the past 10 years, leading to its removal from the theme in October 2020.

Accessing the Theme *via* Funds

Direct access to the theme can be obtained through purchasing shares in the companies in the theme. This can be done through a stockbroking account.

Indirect access to the theme can be obtained in a number of different ways, which may suit some subscribers not wishing to select from the basket of 14 stocks that we provide:

- State Street Global Advisors **SPDR MSCI World Consumer Staples ETF**. The total annual expense ratio is a low 0.30%. The major holdings include Procter & Gamble, Nestlé, PepsiCo, Coca-Cola, Costco, Walmart, and Philip Morris International. It is traded on the London Stock Exchange in dollars (ticker code: WCOS LN) and on the Amsterdam Euronext Exchange in euro (ticker code: WCOS NA). It's an EU-regulated ETF so that an Irish resident is subject to gross roll-up tax rules.

- **Vanguard's Consumer Staples ETF (VDC).** The total annual expense ratio is a low 0.10%. This ETF is listed in the US and therefore subject to the less onerous capital gains tax rules for Irish residents. The main holdings include Procter & Gamble, PepsiCo, Coca-Cola, Costco, Walmart, Philip Morris International, and Mondelēz. As the ETF is listed in the US, it cannot be bought by retail investors in Ireland (as there is no KID available on US ETFs) although it can be bought by an advisor who operates a client account on a 'discretionary' basis.

- **Finsbury Growth & Income Trust (FGT LN).** This is an actively managed investment trust listed on the London Stock Exchange and quoted in sterling (but the underlying assets are not hedged to sterling so that the fund's currency exposure matches that of its underlying holdings). The fund's annual total expense ratio is 0.63%. The major holdings include RELX, London Stock Exchange, Diageo, Burberry, Unilever, Sage, Experian, Mondelēz International, Schroders, and Heineken.

Iconic Consumer Brands for More Defensive, Lower-risk Investing

Annual Review 2023

The Defensive Global Consumer Franchise Stocks Theme offers a balanced alternative between the higher risks associated with general equity investing and the safety of risk-free government bonds.

Companies in the theme own many iconic brands, such as Coca-Cola, Colgate, Listerine, Cadbury, Gillette, Head & Shoulders, Guinness, Heineken, Nescafé, Dove, Vaseline, and Ben & Jerry's.

Their sales and profits tend to be defensive during recessions, because they are essential items, or affordable luxuries. Because they are low-ticket, everyday, repeat purchases, their sales and profits tend to be predictable. And, finally, because they are irreplaceable in consumers' minds, they can often raise prices without losing customers.

Defensive, predictable, and inflation-resistant sales and profits – such enviable attributes! What better way for the risk-averse investor, who nonetheless wants a reasonable return on their capital, to invest?

Gillen.

E: info@gillenmarkets.com
T: +353 1 2871400
W: www.gillenmarkets.com